POSH
OVERNIGHT

THE TEN PILLARS OF
SOCIAL ETIQUETTE

Preface: A Brief Survival Guide for Social Etiquette

Maryanne Parker

Posh Overnight
- The 10 Pillars of Social Etiquette

Maryanne Parker

ISBN-13: 978-1985176409
ISBN-10: 1985176408

TABLE OF CONTENTS

The world was my oyster but I used the wrong fork.

—Oscar Wilde

A Brief Survival Guide for Social Etiquette

Dear reader,

I am so privileged to be able to take you on a journey through the magical world of social etiquette, which was once relevant and accessible only to the chosen ones. From the days of Louis XIV of France to our modern-day manners, etiquette has evolved quite a bit, but there are still many timeless principles that will allow you to never to feel lost and intimidated again.

I would like to tell you how this book came about and why I decided to share it with the world. My last book, *The Sharpest Soft Skill: 10 Proven Etiquette Strategies for Business Success*, was born when I realized that we definitely needed a guide for how to succeed in business and excel in our professional careers based on our "soft skill," emotional intelligence. I agree with great communications experts who advocate that etiquette is the sharpest soft skill: as Mahatma Gandhi said, "In a gentle way, you can change the world."

But what happens after we achieve our initial goals, create and achieve new goals, and we're moving up and up—in our community, our society, nationally, and internationally?

I'll be sharing many personal experiences (some which are faltering or humorous) I've had during my process of learning, growing, and surrounding myself with ultimate sophistication.

Let's face it: most of us are not, and will never be, true English ladies or gentlemen. But wouldn't it be fabulous to raise our standards and live life to the fullest, especially by not feeling intimidated and outcast in certain situations?

This is a hands-on guide to transformation in the fastest and most painless way possible. You won't feel out of place ever again—not while attending dinner parties with your partner or anticipating high-profile events wondering what to wear and what kind of gift to present to the hostess.

If you don't raise your standards, you'll have a mediocre life, and what could be better than reaching your full potential?

After achieving professional success, you need to upgrade your social skills because you'll start to find yourself surrounded by sophisticated, polished, and poised individuals—just like you.

This book will help you learn how to avoid potentially embarrassing moments. This opportunity will open many doors for you; your confidence will skyrocket, and the sky will be the limit.

Please, allow me to invite you on a beautiful journey, from the palace of France's Louis XIV to London's Savoy Hotel and Royal Opera House.

Be *my* guest.

INTRODUCTION

Welcome!

You've made a great decision to learn about proper etiquette, the history of etiquette, and modern-day manners, which are as essential today as they were hundreds of years ago.

Many people say that our society is changing for the worse, and I am on a mission to bring civility back. You will be one of the messengers, spreading the knowledge of etiquette and good manners whenever you go. Not only will your own life change for the better—you'll be widely accepted in many different places—but you'll start changing other people's lives because they will want to spend time with you and be like you—poised, polite, sophisticated, and magnificent.

Modern-day manners are about inclusion. I always say that it doesn't matter where we are coming from; it matters where we are going, and I know from personal experience how true is this.

I came to the United States as a happily married young woman, full of positivity, energy, hope, and faith, eager to experience the American dream.

Eight months later, I found myself with my two children (who were babies at the time) in a homeless shelter for victims of domestic violence. I was somewhere on the central coast of California in a place I'd never heard of before, without any family or friends and with only a limited knowledge of English. I was broken and broke.

What helped me survive was my knowledge of some basic manners, treating people with respect, and building relationships. You do not need a lot to be able to survive, but if you want to raise your standards—and trust me, you do—I'll walk you through some fundamentals.

When you eventually raise your standards, you'll be surrounded by elegant, sophisticated, well-mannered individuals, and you'll want to be like them. You'll want to raise your social status, and when you do, with that territory comes responsibility. People will start watching you all the time. You might think your behavior is impeccable, but if you do one thing incorrectly, they'll remember it.

So let's dive into the world of social etiquette and make some transformational changes together.

Of course, when we think of etiquette, the first name that comes to mind is Louis XIV of France, one of the most successful monarchs of all time. His royal chateau, the Palace of Versailles, was once a very modest hunting estate in the suburbs of Paris.

But the Sun King transformed it in one of the most exquisite historical places in the world. More than three million people visit the Palace of Versailles each year to take in its breathtaking majestic, sophisticated atmosphere. The Palace of Versailles is a preferable destination of choice in any given season!

Louis XIV (1638–1715) was known for his extravagant lifestyle and strict rules of etiquette (some of them stranger than others), and his strategies and clear vision made him one of the most powerful French monarchs in history. His contributions—in terms of history, art, and culture—influenced the rest of Europe and the world.

This magnificent king loved to throw lavish parties and ceremonies at Versailles, but every time he had a party, the palace was turned into a filthy mess. The guests weren't respectful of their surroundings; they littered everywhere. He had to come with a plan of action. Collaborating with his gardener (he had meticulously manicured gardens that could take your breath away, and he was trying desperately to protect them), he started to make little labels, called "etiquettes," that directed people what to do and what not to do, and he placed them around the palace grounds.

This is how etiquette was born. Louis created as many rules as he could (e.g., how to dress in a particular extravagant and expensive way, new dancing steps), and the nobles were obligated to learn them; while they were busy trying to follow all the new guidelines, he was able to keep them under control and prevent any revolutionary ideas. Many of them were also deep in debt because they had to catch up with the modern trends, and this was very expensive.

CHAPTER ONE

How to Be Posh

Learn about the satisfaction that comes from living the good life. After all, as Francis Bacon, English philosopher, scientist, and author said, "Knowledge is power."

Some words in the dictionary do not offer a clear explanation of their roots; such is the case with the word *"posh."* In today's world, posh indicates a luxurious, stylish lifestyle. Back in the day, this kind of lifestyle was typical for those who belonged to "high society." Etiquette then was all about exclusion, which led to extreme social segregation. Today, modern-day etiquette is all about inclusion.

We can implement a posh lifestyle by being polite, well-mannered, classy, and stylish and by learning the main pillars of social etiquette. Being posh today is also a mindset, and we need to be open to new possibilities of learning, increasing our exposure, and raising our standards. Posh could be the short version of "exquisite" or "sophisticated." It's up to us which interpretation we will follow.

Challenge yourself: take five minutes and write down a few positive terms you associate with the word *posh*. Pick the words that best represent your situation and understanding. I've included mine below.

EXERCISE: (write your examples below)

_____

_____

_____

_____

_____

_____

_____

And here a few of mine:

- **_Polite_** – One of the most important requirements of etiquette is being polite. Politeness not only opens every door possible but also shows respect and gratitude to the people we communicate with.

  Maya Angelou said, "I've learned that people will forget what you said, people will forget what you did, but people will never forget how you made them feel." I hope that polite is one of the main words in your representation of what posh means. Being polite means that you genuinely do care about people and you are concerned about their feelings. This means that you need to show respect at any given time, knowing how to react in every single situation and how to be diplomatic.

  Thinking that you have to always tell the truth might not be the best option. Being tactful is extremely crucial in today's society. This shows the level of your social skills. In life, we have to learn to get along with people. Being in conflict is never pleasant, and it's not preferable. Besides, it doesn't make us winners. Our reaction to negativity does.

- *Outstanding* – The next word I associate with being posh is the word "outstanding." How we present ourselves, how we make our initial introduction, what kind of host or guest we are, how we hold a conversation—everything is part of our "package" that makes us irresistible and outstanding.

  Remember: we only have five to ten seconds to make a first impression. It's almost impossible to reverse a negative first impression. It may sound cliché, but it's true; we never get a second chance to make a good first impression.

  "Outstanding," according to the *Free Dictionary*, means "being exceptionally good." Let's face it: our society today is extremely relaxed; people don't pay much attention to good manners, thoughtful communication, treating people with respect, and in general any kind of form of sophistication. As a matter of fact, many people feel awkward when they show simple forms of etiquette.

  You and I should be on a mission to bring good ol' manners back. Even if we feel a bit self-conscious in the beginning, little by little we can change the wrong perceptions and perspectives. Many parents don't have time to teach their kids proper etiquette because we are too busy of rushing through life. Let's stop for a minute and reflect. If we don't, we are looking at future generations with poor manners, which will lead to an even more chaotic, hurtful world. I certainly refuse to live in such a world, and you should feel the same way. (And I know you do if you are reading this book.)
- *Stylish* – Stylishness is a skill that we can develop. We are not just born stylish; we work in this direction, either consciously or not. Being stylish is a complex task. It's not just about our clothing or our appearance; it's also about our lifestyles and manners.

  Being stylish doesn't require a lot of money. Your style defines your personality in a very specific way. Because you are unique, you should have your own memorable (in a positive way) style. Your style is your signature. When you have a specific style that reflects your personality, it's not usually about fashion, because fashion can't really define you.

Of course, when you pay little attention to the latest fashion trends and you really want to be unique, you still have to follow certain standards. For example, dressing in Victorian-style clothing probably isn't the best possible choice for a modern-day lifestyle. There is always a fine line between been unique and being comic.

In many situations, the latest fashion might not be the best choice, either. Fashion changes all the time, and this doesn't help much when you're trying to create your own particular style. The fact that something is extremely fashionable doesn't mean it might be a great fit for you. For example, some of the trendiest colors might not complement your skin tone.

Being stylish means that you learn about yourself, what fits you and what doesn't. Take the time to get to know yourself. When you do, you'll spread your own brand of radiance. People will love what they see, and they'll love to be around you.

- **Humble** – Being humble is paramount to being classy, well-mannered, and stylish. Princess Diana was lovingly called "The People's Princess" in part because she was an icon of humility—beautiful, royal, and extremely humble. This is an incredibly important attribute for any person to possess. Your success and your fortune can skyrocket, and your opportunities and possibilities might be endless, but being humble will make you a flower in the desert! Not being humble strips your success and shows a rather classless portrait of yourself. In many situations, people don't feel accomplished and their self-esteem is pretty low, so they try to compensate for that with an aggressive attitude. Being humble shows vulnerability, and only strong people can show their vulnerable side. Are you one of them?

BEING POSH IS ABOUT FIRST AND LAST IMPRESSIONS: THE 4 PS OF FIRST IMPRESSIONS

1. *Polished* – Being polished is a combination of being classy, refined, and sophisticated, with a keen knowledge of social norms. A polished person has high standards for herself and the people around her. During the rise of the "polite society" in England, ladies from good families attended traditional finishing schools—if they wanted to marry well, of course. Their training included lessons about setting a table, being a gracious guest and a remarkable host, communicating properly, and being a nice companion during tea ceremonies. The payoff was marrying successfully. On the other hand, the "finishing schools" for men were their travels; the traditional Grand Tour, which could last up to a year, allowed them to visit different countries and accumulate knowledge, experience, and exposure to life.

   In modern-day etiquette, being polished is similar to being accomplished, even if the attributes might not be exactly the same. The standards are different: women have careers, and hardly anybody can find the time to go on an international tour for a year. But being polished had a desirable meaning then, and it has a desirable meaning now. We all should follow proper etiquette and use good manners if we want to live in a better world.

2. *Poise* – "For beautiful eyes, look for the good in others; for beautiful lips, speak only words of kindness; and for poise, walk with the knowledge that you are never alone" (Audrey Hepburn).

   Poise is an essential element for creating the finished look we all desire. It's the way we carry ourselves, projecting calm confidence, balance, and composure. It also includes our level of eloquence, both verbal and nonverbal. In some countries—for example, in Latin America and Italy— people gesture frequently when they speak, but in other regions, such as the UK, gesturing is very limited.

How you handle negativity also shows how poised you are. If you control your emotions in every situation and don't attract negative attention, this shows that you have mastered the skills of composure and poise. When we learn patience, we can control our emotions more easily and present ourselves in the best way possible. It's not an easy task to accomplish, and everybody has a different level of ability to handle stressful situations, but it can be learned with practice.

3. ***Posture*** – Why is posture so incredibly important? Because we send subliminal messages with our body language. Your posture reveals more about you than you can imagine. It's a question of repetition and constantly reminding yourself to maintain good posture.

    – ***Your back should be always straight,*** with your shoulders slightly open. There's a fine line between being confident and arrogant. Good posture represents grace and elegance. In one of my classes in London, our teacher offered an incredibly easy but very useful example of how to train ourselves on a daily basis to build good posture. She said, "Always imagine that you have a helium balloon on your shoulders." The little things make the biggest impressions in life. Everything is a pattern, and it shows your willingness to stand out.

    – ***Your chin*** should be very slightly up. If it's up too far, though, you'll look snobbish, out of place, and not very approachable. I'm sure you've seen a lot of videos of Princess Diana. Think of her posture: her chin is never up, but her eyes are; this is a technique we all should learn.

    – ***Your arms*** should be next to your body without a lot of movement like swinging them widely while you're walking. You should project elegance and grace. Your stomach should be pulled in at all times. Your feet can be in front of one another, but not dramatically so. In certain industries, this might be a requirement (in the fashion industry, for example, in order to demonstrate the items in the best way possible), but in everyday life, this way of walking is not acceptable. You shouldn't hurry while you walk, and you should never stomp. Your steps should be small enough to be elegant but not too small to challenge your walking. You need to be composed, elegant, and collected at all times.

– When *sitting,* you should follow the same guidelines. Your posture is extremely important, as is the positioning of your legs: always keep your knees and ankles together. Crossing your legs is not considered sophisticated and classy. In some social circles, it might even be seen as frivolous.

In some cultures, gentlemen can cross their legs, but in other cultures, it's not typical. In some situations, men who cross their legs need to be very mindful (if they conduct business in the Middle East, for example) because if the person sitting opposite can see the sole of their shoe, this can be perceived as very offensive.

This is also true when you are *exiting a car:* you should extend your feet out first, followed by your knees, and they should always remain together. Then you can push your body out.

The same requirement applies when you are *entering* a car. The only difference is that you will have to sit in the car first and then gently and graciously tuck your legs in while not separating them.

– When you *stand up,* you should put one of your legs slightly in front of the other, and your hands should be close to your body, with the fingers touching.

Kensington Palace

4. **Presence** – This means there is *something* about you that makes people notice you. Of course, we all hope we have a positive presence, and we want our vibe to be more than welcome. Our presence is a reflection of our inner energy. If we are open, truthful, charismatic, and welcoming, people will be extremely happy to be around us. If we are constantly gloomy, judgmental, unsatisfied with life, and petty, our presence will still be there, but in a negative way.

   Having a positive presence is a question of choice. Again, we need to know ourselves, and this will be a reflection to the world around us. Being polite, well-mannered, and respectful are a few of the features of having a positive, powerful presence.

   When we meet people (especially for the first time), we need to smile, introduce ourselves politely, and listen to the conversation. We need to ask the proper questions—never too personal. We shouldn't be provocative, and we should make the other person feel at ease. It's all about respect. Having a powerful presence is paramount.

CHAPTER TWO

INVITATIONS AND THANK-YOU NOTES

INVITATIONS

Whether you prefer to throw a party or you're more of a partygoer, both choices require some preparation.

As a guest, your responsibility starts from the moment you receive the invitation. Some invitations will be more formal than others. Either way, if you receive an invitation, you are obligated to respond, based on its requirements. This is because the host needs to make preparations for the party, and it's hard to get an accurate count of the guests if they don't respond or if they respond with a "yes" but don't show up.

Any formal invitation will include:

- **Date**
- **Time**
- **Place**
- **Dress code**
- **RSVP** (*always with a deadline*)

Invitations were a certain requirement during the rise of polite society, and it's a tradition we continue to follow to this day.

When we receive the invitation, we can immediately recognize the importance of the event. We definitely can't attend all the parties in town because of our very busy schedules, but some events might be considered mandatory to attend.

- **Date:** We should save the date on our calendar and keep in mind not to replace the event with something more appealing down the road, especially if we responded to the host with a yes.

  Unfortunately, in these modern times, people don't understand the concept of invitations, and they don't follow the rules. Even after they have RSVP'd to the host, they might not seriously consider attending the event, or they don't follow the requirements about who is allowed at the party and who isn't.

  Crashing a party is never okay; this is an extreme form of breaking etiquette rules. Many people feel that etiquette might be snobbish, unnecessary, and outdated, but how would you feel if you threw a baby shower for a friend, clearly indicating on the invitation that it was for only a certain number of people, and a couple of the guests brought a few extra family members? You wouldn't have enough food or beverages for everybody, and your party, or at least your mood, would definitely be ruined.

- **Time:** Time is one of the most important elements of etiquette and good manners: when you appreciate the value of another person's time, you're showing respect for her. If the invitation indicates 6:00 pm, it could be a bit intrusive if you arrive early—the host is probably still busy organizing details for the party. Being too early is considered rude in the same way that being too late is considered inappropriate.

There is no such thing as being fashionably late; more likely, you'll be perceived as unfashionably poor-mannered, and if you need to make a good first impression, this will ruin your chances. So be on time. In my book on business etiquette, *The Sharpest Soft Skill: 10 Proven Etiquette Strategies for Business Success*, you can find techniques that will help you always be on time, no matter what. Being punctual is a skill, and when you make it a habit, you'll never be late again.

The most formal invitations are usually engraved. Simply by touch, we can sense the importance of the potential gathering or event. The names of invited guests will be engraved on the top left corner. On the bottom left corner will be the RSVP and the return address. On the bottom right corner, you'll find the time and the dress code.

In our changing society, modern-day manners dictate that we should be mindful about how we address the guests. We should use alternatives to gender-specific words because we might have same-sex couples.

In some cases, the invitation may indicate an end time as well; some people might want to stay longer than is appropriate.

Make sure that you spell the names of the recipients correctly and use the proper honorifics. The basic honorifics are:

Mr. – for all gentlemen (family status doesn't matter)

Mrs. – for married women

Miss – for unmarried women (usually for girls under 18 years of age).

Back in the day of the rise of polite society and for a long time after, invitations written to married women were addressed with the name of their husband. For example, if the lady was married to Mr. Frank Jeffrey, her invitation would be addressed to Mrs. Frank Jeffrey. Etiquette is a timeless practice, but it continues to evolve with our ever-changing society and its norms, and certain rules change. The safest choice for a woman may be Ms., but if she prefers to be addressed as Mrs., then we should address her in that way.

In social situations, we don't usually address people by their professional titles, but if we do use the professional title, we should eliminate the social one.

For a comprehensive understanding of names and honorifics, I strongly suggest you read the book *Honor and Respect: The Official Guide to Names, Titles, & Forms of Address* by one of my favorite teachers, Mr. Robert Hickey.

When we address formal invitations, we should be aware that using colorful pencils or pens is not considered formal: it's distracting and playful. You could use them for a children's party invitation, but not for addressing formal adult invitations. I prefer to use dark blue ink (which many people prefer) when I write anything; however, the most formal ink color is black.

If there any specific indications to be addressed and it's not an extremely formal event, we can usually simply share the information over the phone. If pets, kids, or gifts are not expected, we should let the recipient know in advance (in a polite way, of course). Also, there shouldn't be any exceptions—if we tell one family that the party is only for adults, then the "adults only" policy will have to apply for everybody. In this situation, we cannot be selective; that would be extremely rude.

It is the guest's responsibility to follow the instructions on the invitation (if there is a "no gifts" policy, that can usually be indicated over the phone). A no-gift policy should always be followed because most people won't bring gifts, and it would be rude to make them feel uncomfortable just because we decide to bring a gift. However, if we do bring a gift, we should give it to the host very discreetly, without the rest of the guests seeing it.

- **RSVP:** Always make sure to RSVP by the deadline or even a little before. If you confirm your attendance after the deadline, you're already late. Always remember that, after you RSVP, you can't change your plans; not attending has to be the result of a significant event that's out of your control.

  When you RSVP to a formal invitation, the rule is to always send a handwritten response to the host.

THANK-YOU NOTES

The thank-you note is one of the most underappreciated gestures in the manners of modern society. Thank-you notes, contrary to popular belief, are still relevant, especially when done correctly. The thank-you note should be send in a timely manner, preferably 24 to 48 hours after the celebration. For weddings, the rules are a little different.

Sending a thank-you note depending on the formality

The formality of the thank-you note should match the formality of the event. If gifts were involved, always make a specific reference to the gift, and describe how you plan to use it.

Tone of the message

Try to sound sincere when you send a thank-you note, even if it's for a gift you didn't like. Always say that the gift is appreciated and that you will use it. Etiquette is about diplomacy, not hurting the other person's feelings. Sending a thank-you note without any enthusiasm and downplaying the thoughtfulness of the gift is something we should all avoid.

Always send a thank-you note to a thoughtful hostess, especially if she hosted the party in your honor. If you were invited to a dinner, it is not necessary to send a thank-you note, but it is very thoughtful.

Personalizing

Always remember to personalize the thank-you note. A personal touch is essential for everything we do. Sending a generic reply to all of our guests is something we should avoid. Also, we need to consider how close we are to the individuals we are thanking. If they are in our closest circle of friends, we can show more personal appreciation and slight informality. If the recipient of the thank-you note is not in our close circle, we can be more formal.

Of course, in certain societies, even if people saw each other on a daily basis, they still addressed each other in a very formal way. This was perfectly acceptable and sometimes even a requirement.

If you are choosing between expressing your thanks via e-mail, a phone call, or a thank-you note, always choose the thank-you note.

Length

The thank-you note does not have to be long and too explanatory. If we have too many notes to write, we can become overwhelmed and inefficient. We build relationships and connections based on our thoughtfulness. It is always much better to send brief, thoughtful thank-you notes instead of not sending any.

Spelling and grammar

When you send a thank-you note, it is very important to check the spelling of the recipients' names. Also check your grammar. You might be able to send an amazingly charming thank-you note, but if the grammar and spelling are not correct, it could tarnish the message and the gratitude we are trying to convey. Of course, errors can happen, and the recipient shouldn't be petty about them, but we should always take that extra bit of time and try our best.

Always change the thank-you note if you make mistakes that can't be fixed. Thank-you notes with scratched-out words and corrected errors is inappropriate.

CHAPTER THREE

BEING UNFORGETTABLE HOST AND GUEST

Many people love hosting parties for one reason or another. Other people don't like to be the host, but at one time or another, we will all have the pleasure (or necessity) of hosting a party. And we definitely would like to have at least a basic understanding of the rules and norms for doing so. We all have events we just *love* to go to (and others we are just too afraid to attend because we have a bad taste from the last party we were invited to by the very same host). Some parties and events are simply irresistible, thanks to the host or the hostess.

What are the basic requirements for hosting a party?

CREATING A GUEST LIST

If it is a formal dinner, we should not only draft a guest list but also consider creating a sitting arrangement and a menu. Usually, mixing groups of friends we know from different areas of life is not a very good idea. We should try to gather friends who are part of one particular group at the same time. If it is a very special occasion that happens only once, then we can invite everybody, even if they might be part of different social circles. If we are a good hostess or host, after proper introductions, we can make the event memorable for everyone.

In the introductions and sitting arrangements, officials always go before anybody else. The guest of honor always sits on the right side of the host. The host/ hostess should position him/herself in a way to be able to observe the door, especially if there is a catering staff; we should be able to see everything that's going on and what is needed.

It is not polite to ask guests to help with particular elements of the organization of the party. That is the responsibility of the hostess and the host.

1. Plan One – if we have only one host and one guest, the guest should always be seated on the right side of the host.
2. Plan Two – if we have one host and a cohost, the guest of honor sits on the right side of the host, and guest of honor number two sits on the right side of the cohost.
3. Plan Three – if we have six guests, the host and cohost always follow the same requirement: the host sits at the middle of the table, the guest of honor sits on the right side of the host, guest of honor number two sits on the right side of the co-host, guest number three sits on the left side of the host, and guest number four sits on the left side of the cohost, who sits in the opposite direction from the host.

The maximum number of guests seated at the table should be no more than 12, and the space between each of them should be approximately two feet.

4. Plan Four – if we have many guests and we need to position them at different tables, we could avoid placing numbers on the tables and create a different way to recognize the table while the guest goes through the reception table. If numbers are indicated on the tables, this could be perceived as positioning the guests based on importance, which appears inappropriate and offensive. I know many details like this might be not so important to many people, but the atmosphere of the event and the knowledge of the host will determine if we will be returning in the future. The person who introduced the idea of tables without numbering in the United States was Jackie Kennedy.

Mrs. Kennedy also introduced the use of different colors based on the seasons. Back in the day, etiquette dictated that the most formal color for events was white: white tablecloths, white napkins, white candles (which were extremely difficult to produce). Mrs. Kennedy's change was widely accepted.

In historic Great Britain, the hostess and hosts didn't use any tablecloths because they took pride in their furniture, which was probably collected during their travels (such as the Great Tour for men) or had belonged to a family member. Hosts wanted to show their visitors how accomplished they were and that they were part of a prominent family.

CREATING THE MENU

Creating a menu is one of the most important responsibilities for any event, and it might take a long time to be able to fit in the requirements for all our guests. We also have to consider the skills of the staff who will be helping during the event.

CHOICE OF THE EVENT'S STYLE

This usually depends on how much time we might have for this particular event. If we don't have more than an hour, we can simply use a buffet style. Plated dinners require much more attention and involve many more people. We need to consider the venue, the occasion, and the time frame.

ALWAYS CONSIDER DIETARY RESTRICTIONS FOR OUR GUESTS

We have to be aware if any of our quests has any dietary restrictions; it is the duty of the *guest* to inform the host regarding this. In the old style of entertaining, it was almost impossible for the host or hostess to ask the guests if they had any of these kinds of restrictions because it was considered extremely rude to ask personal questions, and health and diet are considered very personal topics, indeed.

In modern-day manners, it is perfectly acceptable for the hostess or the host to have a question regarding any restrictions they might need to know about. Such restrictions might include food allergies, diabetes, lactose intolerance, being vegetarian or vegan, and many others.

A great host should have a few options on the menu for these types of different situations.

RELIGIOUS CONSIDERATIONS

We definitely have to know our guests at least a little bit, because this can help us create an amazing impression as hostess or host. Of course, if the circumstances allow, we should follow any strict religious norms we are aware of.

For example, if the majority of your guests are from the Middle East, you should refrain offering *any* pork or alcohol. Or if your guests are from India, you should consider not serving any beef because the cow is considered a sacred animal in India.

Also, we should plan our party based on the religious calendars of our guests. Again, if our guests are from the Middle East, the month of Ramadan wouldn't be an appropriate time for a party.

TIMELY PREPARATION

We should consider not experimenting during the day of the event. Even if we do have the most impeccable cooking skills, something could always go wrong, and we should prepare dishes we are comfortable and confident in making. Experiments could backfire at the time of the event.

A good host and hostess should create a pleasant atmosphere for the guests. A stressed and overwhelmed host or hostess can bring negative energy to the guests, and this could ruin the party.

The most important part of every successful event is on-time preparation. Don't organize everything at the last moment; this shows poor management skills and almost guarantees a disastrous party.

ALWAYS BE GRACIOUS

When you're hosting an event, your body language says it all. If you're moody, unhappy, and stressed, your guests will pick up that vibe, and the party will be ruined in no time.

I'm sure many of us have a lot of stories to tell, both positive and negative, about good and bad hostesses. I'd like to share a story that didn't only surprise me, it shocked me. Some years ago, my kids and I were invited to a Thanksgiving lunch, and we were really excited to go. My children were young at the time, and they loved playing with the hostess's kids, so we were all expecting to have an unforgettable celebration and to build more memories together.

We went to the party, and soon after we arrived, the hostess went left the room, and we were all just left there with her family. We didn't know what happened. It was a very uncomfortable situation, because I didn't know her husband or the rest of her family very well. We hadn't been there that long, either. After suffering a while in those awkward circumstances, we decided to leave, of course, and we couldn't even say goodbye or thank you to our hostess because she wasn't around. She hadn't excused herself or informed us that she needed to step out for some time. She had just left, and no one knew what happened.

The next day, she sent an e-mail and apologized to all of us who had attended the party, saying that she had felt tired due to the preparation for the holiday. We received invitations in the future from her, but I politely refused all of them.

The bottom line is: poor organization usually leads to poor performance. I understand things can happen, but the polite hostess never leaves her guests for an extended time. At the very least, she should walk them out. Being a host carries a lot of responsibility, and if you don't have the energy or desire to do certain things, your best bet is probably not to organize an event in the first place.

Some hostesses are so concerned about the tidiness of the setting that they forget to make the guests feel comfortable. Yes, the house will probably get a little messy and some glasses of wine might get spilled, but that's not a reason to ruin your own party. When she sees that you spilled your glass of red wine on her 100-year-old white tablecloth, a good hostess will spill her own wine intentionally, just to keep you from being uncomfortable.

BEING UNFORGETTABLE GUEST

Our responsibility starts when we receive an invitation to attend an event, dinner party, or any kind of occasion. Most important, we should follow the requirements on the invitation regarding RSVP, dress code, etc.

Assume that we did accept the invitation, and the time of the event is here. The first responsibility we have is to arrive on time. Being too early is intrusive; being too late is rude. So try to be there on time. Of course, if there is some unavoidable delay—heavy traffic, for example—arriving a little later can be acceptable.

Try not to rush for the event. Leave yourself plenty of time to get ready. For the ladies, especially if you know that your hair or makeup might take longer than usual, make sure to give yourself the extra time you need.

Always dress to impress, and if it is a formal event, follow the requirements on the invitations. We will talk about dress code in detail in chapter 6.

When you attend an event, you'll need to know how to make the right entrance and how to present yourself in the best way possible. Being poised, polite, and irresistible is a skill, and if we would love to be remembered in the best way possible, we will have to learn the skill of etiquette. For example, what are the appropriate topics of conversation, and why?

GIFT GIVING AND RECEIVING

Should you bring gifts, and if so, what kind? It depends on the occasion. Usually, when we attend a private event like a dinner party or a family celebration, we bring gifts, unless the invitation indicates otherwise.

Also, when you visit anybody's home for the first time, it's a thoughtful gesture to bring a gift.

Bringing a gift shows consideration, appreciation, respect,
and positive thoughts.

The gift giving should be done in a tasteful manner. You always need to consider the fact that the gift giving is never about you; it's always about the host—their needs, desires, and personality. If you don't know much about your host, try to pick up something simple, uncontroversial, and truly meaningful, such as a something for house decoration, a book, or a plant. You could bring a bottle of wine, which is great for traditional gatherings in the US or in Europe. If your host's religion forbids alcohol, familiarize yourself up front and bring something else.

Always try to wrap your gift properly and nicely. Using Christmas wrapping paper for an Easter celebration won't present you in the most favorable way possible. The presentation is always in the details. Of course, you always can use color coordination and some festive decorations to make it look beautiful.

If you are attending a nice celebration, gift cards are not the best choice. You can bring a gift card *in addition* to a special gift, but gift cards alone are not considered meaningful and thoughtful. It looks as though you didn't take the time to choose a personal gift for your host.

If it's a more personal atmosphere (such as a family gathering for Christmas) and you're not sure the recipients will like your gifts (or fit into them), you can leave the receipt in the box so they can exchange the item. This is *only* for your close circle: family members and friends. Otherwise, leaving the receipt inside the gift is considered a faux pas.

Re-gifting is also an option for certain situations. This is acceptable only if the gift has never been opened, never been used, and looks brand-new. Otherwise, it is definitely better not to give anything. Above all, make sure the recipient is not in the same circle of close friends or family members as the person who originally gave you the gift!

Your gift should be always appropriate and, as I said before, uncontroversial, because you don't know how it might be perceived.

Also, the price range has to be taken into consideration. The reason for this is that, usually, after we receive a gift we should reciprocate. If you present an expensive gift to your host, you might make them uncomfortable because they can't return the favor in terms of price range. Try to find out the price range for gifts, based on the occasion.

The host should always accept the gift graciously, never showing disappointment even if she doesn't like it or doesn't consider it useful. The gift should be treated with special care when it's received. One of the most important elements of etiquette is to handle our emotions accordingly and properly. We always need to stay collected and classy.

The moment you make your entrance, you should greet your host, and be brief about it. You definitely shouldn't occupy the host's attention consistently and intrusively, because you won't be the only one invited.

When you enter the room or the hall, step out on your right or left (just don't stay at the door, blocking the other guests from getting in). When you step aside, you'll have a moment to collect yourself and collect many useful details: who is at the event, how many people are there, where the bar is (☺), and who you know.

If it is a big event, you will be ready to meet a lot of people. Always be poised and polished when you introduce yourself.

INTRODUCTIONS

At some high-profile events, you will have to rely on the host to introduce you to some of the other attendees or to the guest of honor. On these occasions, it could be inappropriate and rude for you to take the introduction in your own hands, but in the US, on most occasions it's fine to introduce yourself.

The introduction is one of the most important first contacts between you and the person in front of you. Don't introduce yourself with only with your first name. Always introduce yourself with your first and last name.

My name is Bond. James Bond.

If the person doesn't understand your name immediately, make sure to correct him gently; assume the responsibility if he didn't understand the first time. Self-deprecation is a useful technique. For example, you could say, "I am sorry. Sometimes my accent gets in my way" (something I would say, for example) or "I am sorry. I should have spoken a little louder" or "I should have spoken clearer."

In our American culture, we should always make eye contact while introducing ourselves. Eye contact should be firm and never too long and intrusive. Eye contact is very important because it shows that you are present and genuinely interested in meeting the person. It also shows a lot of confidence and gives off a good vibe.

Proper introductions are always made when you are standing. Sitting down and introducing yourself is not polite in our time of modern-day manners. Back in the day, it was perfectly fine for ladies to be introduced while they sat, but in today's society, the only time this is acceptable is if you are "trapped" for some reason (such as between the chair and the table).

Always extend your hand for a handshake. The handshake should be firm. In social situations, you can have a moderately firm handshake, but in business situations, you should have a very firm handshake (see *The Sharpest Soft Skill*).

When you meet people, always smile—send those good positive vibes to everyone you meet. Hold your drink in your left hand—you'll be shaking people's hands with your right hand, and it's always good for that hand to be clean, not slippery, wet, and cold.

MINGLING

If you want to join a group of people, do it politely. Just ask, "May I join you?" I don't think anybody will ever say no. However, don't ask to join a group of just two people. They might be having a personal conversation, and it might be uncomfortable for you to join them.

Not all of us can be incredible conversationalists, but good encounters start with just that—a conversation. Be friendly (even funny), open, interesting, and interested. Always start with light topics, not controversial ones. Avoid politics, religion, and money, just as the old saying goes. If you have a strong opinion on something, try not to advocate for it at that very moment. You never know what the outcome might be.

Always remember to have at least five topics for small talk. Of course, to be able to lead or handle conversations well, one of the requirements is that you be informed. You don't need to know everything, but you need to know *something*. People don't need statistical details, but basic knowledge of the world and the things that interest the people around you will help you any time you want to be a part of an interesting group.

You can talk about books, travel, food, local places, or sports—always green-light territory when done correctly. Leave out personal questions. Some people are more discreet than others, and the particular event might be not the best place for you to try and change their views on one topic or another.

Always try to taste everything, or almost everything, from the food offered by the host. Of course, if there is anything you *really* don't like or you're allergic to, just politely refuse to eat it. If there is something that you'd rather not try, just say so, but in an appropriate way. Don't explain yourself; just say "No, thank you," and that should be enough. I had a very unfortunate situation when I was on a vacation in South Africa. I was invited to a high-profile event, and the menu was incredible. The host had traditional tastes, and there were fried caterpillars on the menu. I was extremely timid at the time, and I couldn't refuse this local delicacy, even though it was something I wasn't prepared to try, let's say, *ever*! They had preplated my food, and I couldn't eat anything throughout the evening. I was extremely hungry at the end, and I hope the host didn't feel bad because I didn't try the caterpillars.

If you're attending an event that has a help staff, you have the right to be there, but by all means, do *not* give orders to the staff. Remember, you're the guest!

FLOWER ARRANGING

Flowers are a living representation of nature's beauty, and they are part of almost every event or celebration we will attend. Every host and hostess likes to have a nicely decorated table, and every domestic queen likes to impress her guests or spouse by preparing gorgeous environments. There are a few guidelines we should follow when we use flower arrangements for a particular occasion.

Usually, one of the most important requirements for an arrangement of flowers on a table is that it is the appropriate height, not blocking the guests from communicating to each other. The flowers create a beautiful personality and atmosphere. The table flowers are usually used as a centerpiece, if it is a round table. If you have a long table, you can create a few different flower arrangements and place them along the length of the table. I personally like flat bowls with a single flower dropped inside.

You can use almost anything that grows in your garden. Almost anything that has leaves can be used for decorations. Be inspired by the season. If you are arranging a table in the fall, use warmer colors like orange, brown, yellow, and gold. These colors create a warm, welcoming atmosphere. During the winter, you can use dark green that matches the color of your Christmas tree.

For spring, use a lot of green to signify the beginning of the new year and bring a lot of fresh atmosphere. For summer, use a lot of bright colors that complement the golden hues of the sun.

In some cases, you can match the flowers with the colors of the walls or the rug.

Always use flowers with a soft scent, because a strong odor can interfere with the aroma of the food on the table. You don't want all that delicious food you prepared to smell like gardenias! In addition, some of your guests might get a headache or experience allergies to strong-scented flowers.

In some cultures, even numbers represent death. For example, where I am from originally (Bulgaria), even numbers of flowers are used for funeral arrangements. Make sure to do your research whenever you use flowers, because if you have guests from different cultures, you don't want them to be reminded of a sad occasion, so you'll probably have to make some changes.

The color of the flowers could have negative meanings in some cultures as well. For example, in China and some other Asian countries, white is the color for sad occasions. In some European countries, the color yellow represents envy. The magic is in the details, and everything can have a subliminal effect.

Flowers' symbolism has existed for centuries. According to *Living Arts Original* (a website I stumbled upon some years ago), the meaning of flowers was widely developed and used during the Victorian era. There was a strict protocol when it came to communicating emotions, and thoughts were often expressed only in a coded way, through flowers. Sometimes a bouquet or a single bloom represented something in particular, depending on the flower, the color, or the number. Flowers are still used to represent emotions today. For example, red roses represent romance.

When you are the guest and you want to bring flowers, always make sure to bring them in a beautiful vase. You don't want to create more work for the hostess—she doesn't need to start looking for a vase for your flowers when you arrive.

CHAPTER FOUR

FINE DINING ESSENTIALS

THE MEANING OF THE TABLE

E very celebration, every triumph, every family bonding ritual takes place at the table. The table setting can be formal or informal. We all know about informal dining, when we're all in a rush, sitting in front of the TV, and passing time. What if, instead, we took the time to enjoy every moment, build memories, hear interesting stories, create unforgettable relationships, and taste foods we have never knew about before?

The table has a deep meaning besides just being a place to eat. In England, during the rise of polite society, tables were a symbol of the endless stories and rich experiences from the gentlemen's Grand Tours. The tables could have beautiful ornaments and carvings, and they were probably brought from faraway locations. Each table had its own story to tell. Many times, in most aristocratic homes, the table represented success and prestige. The table wasn't covered with a tablecloth because it was a symbol of that particular family's lifestyle.

TABLECLOTHS

In this day of modern manners, we usually use a tablecloth. The most formal tablecloths are white and long. Some of them can be carried through generations, which means that we as guests should be really careful not to spill anything on them. The shorter and more colorful the tablecloth is, the less formal.

Jackie Kennedy introduced colorful tablecloths and plates because she wanted to create a more festive, distinctive atmosphere. She was an incredibly creative host.

On the table, we usually don't display all the silverware at once, because if we have eight courses, the table will be covered with silverware, and it will be difficult to navigate all those utensils. In addition, with modern-day etiquette, many people could feel extremely out of place. If there are already a few courses on the table and you need an additional knife for your steak, for example, the knife will be placed in front of you a little bit before the steak arrives.

You usually have a charger plate and the service plate in front of you. The charger is usually used to serve your cocktail or soup, and after that, it will be removed. Don't eat from the charger plate. It's just there as an ornament.

NAPKINS

A well-organized host will prepare napkins for their guests. The napkin is in front of every guest, more often on the left side of your charger plate. The napkin is used to keep you clean and to prevent spills on your clothes. The proper way to use the napkin is by putting it gently on your lap with the folded part closer to your torso. Always wait for a signal from the host to start eating. Shortly before that, you can put your napkin on your lap.

Use the napkin only to dab your mouth. When you take a bite and want to have a sip of a drink, the proper etiquette is to dab your mouth before you take a sip, because you don't want to leave an oily stain on the beautiful glass.

Don't use the napkin to wipe your mouth roughly, removing your lipstick. Never spit unwanted pieces of food in it, and never use it to wave at the waiter. For the gentlemen, please don't tuck the napkin in your collar.

You don't have to sit at the table and place the napkin on your lap right away. You can have a short conversation with the people around you, and *then* place the napkin on your lap. Many people believe you should place the napkin immediately after you are seated, but actually, it's your choice. You don't want to look confined and uncomfortable.

When you're done with the meal, fold the napkin slightly, covering the stains and the spills, and leave it on the left side of your plate. Many people leave the napkin on the seat of the chair, but the most hygienic way is to leave it on the table.

Etiquette evolves constantly, and we just need to know basic rules to be comfortable and not to feel like an outcast. Many people feel uncomfortable and intimidated by the prospect of navigating a table setting. They're afraid they'll make a bad impression with their future mother-in-law, fiancé, or the new boss. Don't be one of them. The table shouldn't intimidate you.

When you're sitting at the table, you have to make sure that your posture is straight. Your posture is one of the elements that define your refinement. It's not easy to have good posture; it takes a lot of reminders from a young age, a lot of self-control, and a willingness to present yourself in the best way possible. Also, we all know that elbows shouldn't be on the table. Make sure that you aren't taking up a lot of space. Back in the day of traditional finishing schools, one of the requirements was for the girls to hold books under their arms and to try and eat without dropping them. If they opened their arms too widely, the book would drop, and that was considered incorrect.

After you leave the table, especially in a private home, always remember to push the chair back under the table.

CONVERSATIONS AT THE TABLE

When you have conversations at the table, divide your attention equally between the people on your left and the people on your right. It is very rude to communicate with the person on only one side, regardless of the topic. Don't turn your back to any of your neighbors at the table. If you would like to talk to somebody who isn't right by you, don't shout or scream. This is extremely intrusive to the rest of the people at the table.

Always remember to keep the conversation light and pleasant. Try to talk about beautiful, uncontroversial topics. Try to refrain from talking about politics, religion, and money. If someone attempts to engage you in a provocative topic, try to avoid conflict at all times. Redirect the conversation and be the "bigger person." You do not need to answer. Personal questions can be rude and inappropriate.

Always maintain eye contact and look engaged. Not all topics will be interesting, but we can still engage in them. Always try to listen more instead of talking and trying to be the center of the attention. There is always that one person who monopolizes the conversation. Everybody has something interesting to share, so definitely get involved; just don't dominate the discussion.

THANKING THE WAIT STAFF

When the wait stuff comes, you can thank them once or twice, but not every time they bring you something. The best service in the manor houses was so impeccable that the butlers were almost invisible. If a guest showed appreciation every single time they attended to their needs, it meant that they were not doing their job well; in other words, they were intrusive to a certain extent.

The food is usually served from the left, and beverages are always served from the right. If you are not sure what to do, just sit up straight, without unnecessary movements, until you are served.

Condiments

There will be salt and pepper shakers, and in some establishments, there will be a salt cellar, from which you can spread a little salt on your plate. It is easy to control how much you put on your food. Don't put salt and pepper on your food before you taste it; this is a rude gesture toward the hostess. If anybody asks for the salt or the pepper, always hand them the salt and the pepper together. Do not pass only the salt or only the pepper.

If you'd like a second serving of bread from the basket on the table, offer the basket first to your neighbors on your right and left and in front of you. Then you can take more bread from the basket.

YOUR PHONE AT THE TABLE

There's a popular meme circulating around that asks, "Where do we put our phone—on the left or on the right at the table?" The answer is—neither. We know etiquette evolves over time, but your phone has no place at the table. Put it in silent mode, or better yet, leave it in your car or your purse. While you're at the table, your purpose is to communicate with others and to be present. Of course, urgent things can come up, and if you absolutely have to answer a call, then go ahead and do so. Excuse yourself, leave the table, and take the call. But before you do, let the people around you know that you are expecting a phone call that can't be missed.

Your phone simply doesn't havew a place at the table.

Sending text messages or e-mails, chatting on Facebook, and, especially, cell phone conversations are highly inappropriate while you're at the table.

What else is not permitted on the table?

The only things permissible on the table are the cutlery, napkins, table decorations, and, of course, the food. Anything else simply doesn't belong. This includes ladies' purses. They should be under the table. If you have a clutch, it can stay on your lap. You shouldn't leave your purse hanging on the chair because it might get in the way of the wait staff or your hostess while they serve the food.

Do not leave any medications, books, working supplies, etc., on the table. Everything has a time and place. If you need to take medications, do it before or after the meal. If it's something urgent, excuse yourself and leave the table in order to keep the attention away from you.

And ladies, don't apply makeup at the table. It's not appropriate.

FORMAL DINING

We live in casual times, and many people prefer to dine informally, sitting at home, in a small casual gathering, or even in front of the TV. I encourage you to create a special atmosphere every once in a while; treat yourself and your family to the pleasant, sophisticated, and exciting atmosphere of fine dining. You don't have to have the most expensive china in the world to experience a beautiful evening. Try to use all the beautiful disheswww you received as a gift back in the day or the ones you purchased for a special occasion. Use them now! Tomorrow is never promised, so *today* is a special occasion, and *you* are special as well. Create the style you always wanted for you and your family.

If you're at a high-profile event, everything will be organized to the extreme, and you'll find yourself navigating a labyrinth of silverware. One of the most important rules (after the hostess indicates that you can start the meal) is to **navigate the table setting from *outside in, never from inside out.***

If you're the one who does the placement of the cutlery, be aware that if there will be more than three courses, don't place the entire cutlery on the table at once—never more than twelve utensils at one time. You should place the utensils as they're needed, when each new dish is presented.

Knives are always presented on the right side, with the blade facing in. (Never out, because it looks aggressive, and this is the etiquette rule.)

There is a charger placed on the table, and this plate is for decoration. If there is soup or a cocktail to begin the meal, the staff will place the soup bowl or cup on top of the charger, and after you're done with it, the wait staff will remove everything.

THE FORK
The fork was invented much later than the knife and the spoon. Before the fork was accepted as a utensil, people mainly used a knife. The fork made a slow entry into Europe.

The rule for placing forks is that they always stay on the left side. The only fork that can be placed on the right side is the cocktail fork. Usually inside the soup spoon.

Cocktail fork

Today, we have many different kinds of forks: meat fork, salad fork, cocktail fork, snail fork, asparagus fork, crab fork, pickle fork, ice cream fork, etc., just for our own amusement and convenience (or inconvenience).

At times, this can be a little intimidating. However, if you're reading this book, you're on the right path toward raising your standards, and you already know that the table setting shouldn't intimidate you. Ever!

BREAD PLATE AND BREAD KNIFE

The bread plate is always situated on the left side of the charger plate. You can always use the BMW logo as a reminder—bread, main course, water— or the B and D sign, which I always recommend to the younger students. If you do forget where your bread plate is, you can make a little B and D sign under the tablecloth and remind yourself.

Always remember to break the bread that is offered on the table. Never cut the bread, and never bite from the bread. Simply break off little pieces, one at the time. Spread a little butter on one small piece of bread, and this is the way to eat it. There is usually a butter knife provided with the butter, placed on the plate.

THE GLASSES

Glasses are always placed on the right side of the charter plate. Usually the glasses are positioned as follows: water goblet, white wine, red wine, champagne, and sherry glass. The wine is poured into the glass until it's one-third full. Glasses should be clear for us to be able to see the drink. The beverage is always paired with the menu that is served.

WHITE WINE

White wine is usually served with lighter meals; it is very popular for pairing with fish. The weather can also be a factor—it's usually used during the warmer months. The glasses used for white wine are narrow, just as shown in the picture. White wine is served chilled, but there is a limit: don't leave your white wine in the freezer. This will damage the taste terribly.

RED WINE

Red wine is usually poured into an oval glass, and the temperature is always room temperature or between 60–65 degrees. Red wine need more room to breathe. The taste of the wine can change dramatically if it is served too cold or too warm. I've had the opportunity to live in wine regions, such as Cape Town, one of the most popular destinations for wine experts in the world, and California, which is one of the biggest producers of wine in the world.

CHAMPAGNE

Champagne is usually served in a flute (on the right picture below). Lighter champagne, which is in a wider glass (as shown in the first picture below), is usually served at the very beginning of a meal or as an aperitif before the dinner.

Champagne flute

"Do you know the Bishop of Norwich?" or how you serve port

First, a little history of port wine, also known as porto, or port. This is a Portuguese fortified wine from the variety of sweet dessert wines. Usually, the port should be decanted before it has been served; according to wine experts, this brings out the both the aroma and the flavor of the wine.

Port is part of the social scene and enjoyment at many parties where it is served; as a matter of fact, there is an interesting game where everybody gets involved and participates.

What are the rules?

The port starts with the host, who pours the port into the glass of his neighbor on the right. After that, it's passed to the guest on the left, who pours some for the person to the right, and so on until everyone at the table has been served.

When there is a request for a second serving, the guest who wants to have more port should ask the question, "Do you know the Bishop of Norwich?" This is a signal for the port to be passed again.

In some cases, people who are not really experienced in this social game of port etiquette might respond honestly, "No, I am afraid I do not know the Bishop of Norwich."

And the funny answer is: "The Bishop is a terribly good chap, but he never passes the port!" which leads to another round of passing the port.

TOAST ETIQUETTE

There are two main types of toasts:

- a welcome toast (if you are the host), which is usually before the meal, and
- a toast to the guest of honor, which is usually before the dessert. The guest of honor should always reciprocate the thoughtfulness and thank the host with a toast.

BASIC KNOWLEDGE:

1. The toast should be short and to the point. Have you been in a situation when everybody is waiting patiently (or not so), just to have a sip, because the person who initiated the toast forgot about everybody else in the room? Say "I" in Tony Robbins's voice ☺.
2. If you are initiating the toast, you should stand up and gently gather the attention of everyone around. (Do not yell, scream, and tap the glass with your fork!)
3. Do not ever drink in your own honor (this is really bad form).
4. Accept the toast politely by saying "thank you." (Don't start giving all the excuses in the book for why you don't deserve the toast. You are special, and you do deserve it.)
5. You do not have to stand up when you are accepting the toast.

6. Contrary to popular belief, you should not clink glasses. If the glasses are made of expensive crystal, they might easily break (so choose your battles). Of course, if you're in an intimate environment with your friends and someone initiates glass clinking, go for it!

7. Don't ever toast with an empty glass. If you don't drink alcohol, use a different beverage.

MORE CUTLERY

As I mentioned previously, navigate the table from the outside in. The soup spoon is on the right side. It is round and larger than a regular spoon because you drink the soup from the spoon.

Sometimes, if we have a cocktail, the only fork that is on the right is the cocktail fork, and it is positioned next to the soup spoon.

If there is fish on the menu, you will have a fish knife, which is much different than the rest of the knives.

The fish knife is used to initially remove the skin and bones from the fish. Hold it like a pencil, not like a regular knife.

Fish knife

The salad knife is smaller than the regular knife. Sometimes the salad might be served in the beginning of the meal, and at other times after the main course, depending on cultural differences in different countries.

You will see that you have a spoon and a fork above your plate. Never use them during the meal. They are placed there to be used for dessert. Usually, we do slide the fork and spoon down, with the fork on the left and the spoon on the right.

SERVING ORDER

Usually, the dishes are passed on the right, but sometimes someone might start passing the food on the left. You should always follow one direction. Also, if you are serving anything with a handle, turn it around and pass the dish with the handle pointing toward the other person. This is polite, and the person next to you will appreciate the gesture.

During formal meals, you should follow the order of precedence. Ladies are served first, starting with the lady on the right side of the hostess, and after that, the lady on the left side of the hostess. Serving ends with the lady of the house after all of the ladies are served, and then the men are served.

Before the dessert is served, you should always clear the table of the salt, pepper, butter, and all condiments. This creates enough space for the dessert and an appealing atmosphere to enjoy the last part of the meal.

FINGER BOWL

Finger bowls are usually presented when you've had a messy meal, and before the event continues, everyone should use them.

Usually, there is a flower or a lemon slice in the bowl. Dip your fingers (hand after hand), and wipe your hands on your napkin (which is on your lap) gently and unobtrusively.

AMERICAN STYLE OF DINING:

ZIG-ZAG

The American style of dining is the style that was initially used in Europe. This is the natural way to navigate the table setting. The main difference is that during the meal, the knife lies on the edge of the plate, and you switch the fork from the left to the right hand. Use the knife with the fork while cutting your food. After you cut a bit of food (for example, a small piece of meat), switch. The knife is always blade in. The fork should be held by the hand you are more comfortable using. The fact that the fork is usually on the left side doesn't mean that you have to use that hand if you are not comfortable doing so.

The way to hold the knife is with the index finger on the handle, never on top of the blade. Always cut one piece at a time, and eat a bit from everything on the plate.

We also call this style zig-zag because we switch the fork from one hand to the other. This is a much easier and more natural way to use utensils.

Resting position:

Simply leave the knife on the edge of the plate (right side, top) and the fork inside the plate. We call this "silent service code" because you don't need to explain it to the wait staff or the hostess; they can simply see it.

When we are done with our food, we leave the fork and the knife next to each other with the tines up at 6/12 or 10/4.

Even though we're probably most familiar with the American style of dining, most of the world uses the Continental style.

CONTINENTAL STYLE OF DINING

We already know that etiquette was used as a means of exclusion back in the day. Some rules were more obscure than others, and the Continental style was born. With this style, you usually do not switch hands while using the fork. Your knife is also used as a pusher in addition to cutting the food. So, with the knife, you can put different pieces of food on top of the fork: if you eat meat, you can cut one piece at a time, push a small piece of potato on top of it, and then eat it. This is a way to eat even the smallest pieces of food properly.

TAKING A BREAK

It's natural to take a break from your food now and then to take a sip from your beverage or to have a conversation with your neighbor, starting from the left and ultimately with your neighbor on the right.

Always remember not to put used utensils back on the table-cloth; they should always stay on the plate. Here's the proper way to do it: simply make a little space on your plate, and place the utensils crossed *inside* the plate. Don't leave the utensils sticking out of the plate like boat vessels, because they can easily fall down, and it's not the appropriate way to do it. The following picture indicates a wrong positioning of the utensils.

And finishing position:

When you'd like to indicate that you're done with your meal, simply put the utensils next to each other in a 6-12 or 10-20 position, with the tines down.

The fork tines will face down, just like in the picture below.

While taking a break, place your napkin on the left side on the table. Try to fold it gently and not to show the soiled parts of it.

We already spoke about the positioning of the cutlery and how to use the utensils. Now it's time to use our knowledge.

I mentioned before that you should wait for the hostess to let you know when you can start eating.

Always remember that your elbows never go on the table. Eat with your mouth closed, and don't talk until you've swallowed your food. When you'd like a sip of your beverage, wipe your mouth gently, more slightly; dab your mouth. Remember your posture, don't sit too close or too far from the table, and remember the BMW rule.

ENGLISH TABLE

Forks and spoons are in open positions, and the tines of the forks are facing upwards. Also, the dessert utensils are placed on top of the plate. The napkin is placed on the bread plate. Traditionally, the reason why the cutlery was always facing up was because the name of the family was engraved on them, and this was a way to show how important they were in the society.

FRENCH TABLE

Forks and spoons are in a closed position, and tines are always facing down. This was what Louis XIV requested from his court because he was extremely paranoid about violence, which could jeopardize his life. Also, during Louis XIV's reign, French fashion was very glamorous, and clothing had a lot of mainsheets and long, hanging sleeves, so it could be extremely uncomfortable to have the tines up. In the French table setting, we usually have the glasses on the top part of the plate, placed in a row.

Usually on very formal occasions, we can withdraw to the drawing room, where we can receive coffee and liqueurs and the gentlemen smoke cigars.

The pouring of the coffee is the indication of the end of a party.

HOW TO EAT SOUP

SOUP COURSE

The soup course is one of the most challenging because many people do not know how to eat soup properly. The soup might be served in a bowl or in a soup plate; if it is in a bowl, it usually comes with a supporting plate underneath. Don't leave your spoon inside the bowl if you take a break, because it might easily spill. Instead, leave it on the supporting plate. If you are served on a larger soup plate, you can leave the spoon inside the plate during a break.

Make sure not to blow on your soup if it is too hot. Simply wait for it to cool off. If the bowl has handles (as it will in some cases, for broth and light bouillon), feel free to use the handles and drink the soup. Analyze the situation; know the rules, because you can use your knowledge to feel comfortable at the table.

Food is always served from the left and cleared from the right, but this is not the case with soup. Soup is served from the right and cleared from the right.

To eat soup, place your spoon (which is round) in the middle of the bowl and start scooping the soup from the middle, away from you. You can gently touch the rim of the opposite side of the bowl, trying to clear every drip left there, and then bring it up to your mouth. Never go down to the food; bring everything up to your mouth. Always sit up straight, and don't slouch.

HOW TO EAT DIFFICULT FOODS

Many times, we will be in situations where we are offered messy foods and we won't know how to handle them. Actually, if you are at a high-profile event, I doubt that such food will be offered to you, but in case you are, I will give you a few etiquette tips.

Foods with pits – When you have food with pits, you will have to find a way to take it out of your mouth in an elegant way. Many etiquette experts suggest that the way the food enters the mouth is the way it should exit. So, you can cover your mouth for a moment, spit the pit onto your fork, and leave it on the side of your plate. Or if you have a special plate for it, you can leave it there.

Dish with shared dips or sauce – In many situations, we're served dishes with shared sauce. The most important thing to remember is that you can't double dip, because it's not hygienic. What should you do? Put some of the sauce on your plate, and then you can dip as much as you want to.

Wings and ribs – These foods are meant to be eaten by holding them with your hands, not with silverware, which means that they will be extremely messy! If you decide to order these in a restaurant, you will have to have request wet wipes or a bowl of water to wash your hands afterwards.

Not a good choice for a formal dinner.

Spaghetti is also considered a messy, difficult to eat food because the sauce could splash everywhere, and people have a tendency to slurp the noodles until they get them all into their mouth. Well, this is a big no-no. What should you do instead? You should cut the spaghetti into manageable portions, twist them around your fork, and eat them that way. Always keep the portions a manageable size.

EATING DESSERT

During dessert, we usually have a knife and fork situated above the plate setting, and the fork is usually under the spoon. They are small and easy to use for pudding or dessert. Dessert is usually served with coffee or tea. The fork is used as an anchor, and the spoon is the main utensil to use for dessert.

In very high-end restaurants, the wait staff might even slide down the fork and the spoon on both sides (left and right) on the dessert plate.

Always leave your utensil inside the plate, never on the tablecloth. Eat slowly, and make sure that you do not finish before everyone else. Take your time, of course, to make sure that you are at the appropriate pace with everyone else.

If you have pudding presented in a form like the one shown in the picture below, do not leave your spoon inside when you are resting from it because it will spill.

COFFEE

Coffee is typically offered at the end of the meal. In the American style of fine dining, the coffee cup is usually always on the table. If you don't want coffee, just tell the waiter; do not turn your cup upside down. Just communicate your request. Coffee mugs are currently popular, but if you have a better option, try to refrain from using them. A little sophisticated coffee cup is enough to make anybody's day and to make you feel good about yourself. It is much more elegant to have your coffee in an appropriate coffee cup. Take your time and enjoy the beverage.

There is usually a small spoon for the sugar, which you can use to put some in your cup. Always stir with a different spoon, then place the spoon on the saucer. If there is a creamer, always offer it first to the people around you, and then you can serve yourself. For the ladies, if you're wearing lipstick, make sure to use only one side of the coffee cup, because it is much more appealing. Nobody enjoys seeing lipstick stains on a coffee cup.

CHAPTER FIVE

CAVIAR: THE ROYAL DELICACY

Caviar has been always of a fascination of mine. I always associated caviar with a beautiful, glamorous, posh lifestyle and events that are strictly reserved for the very rich.

I decided to learn a little more about caviar and to unravel the mystery of why caviar maintains its place as one of the most expensive, lucrative pleasures on earth.

Caviar didn't become expensive only recently; it was also very expensive in Russia and some Middle Eastern countries back in the day, and it was often strictly reserved for royalty.

The word "caviar" originates from the Turkish word "khavyar," which refers to fish eggs extracted from wild sturgeon in the Caspian and the Black Sea. Other types of fish eggs are not considered true "caviar" but are roe or, simply, fish eggs.

The price of caviar can reach up to thousands of dollars. Why is it so expensive? Because it is produced from an old, primitive-looking fish that loves extremely cold water.

It takes more than twenty years for the fish to mature. This particular fish can be found in the Caspian Sea.

There are four kinds of fish that produce authentic caviar. Most of the information that follows regarding the different kinds of fish comes from Wikipedia.

TYPES OF CAVIAR

BELUGA

This particular fish produces one of the most expensive caviars in the world. Some experts estimate that price might go up to $500 per ounce.

The beluga has round, clear, soft eggs. They're relatively large—the size of a pea. The color varies from gray to almost black, and the taste is full and well developed. The distinguishing element of beluga caviar eggs is the dot on the egg. The smell is not strong: it has more of a light fishy smell, but it isn't near the foul smell of a fish.

OSETRA

Osetra caviar is another favored type of caviar. Caviar lovers prefer the smooth, lush taste of this caviar. The color has more earth tones, including yellow, brown, and gold.

This fish can live up to 50 years, grows to be quite large, and re-produces slowly.

SEVRUGA

Sevruga sturgeon is on the smaller side, and its color comes from the fifty shades of grey. This is one of the saltiest caviars of all, and it has a rich flavor. This caviar is not as expensive as the ones mentioned above because the fish can reproduce in seven years, relatively faster than the Beluga and the Osetra, but it's also delicious.

STERLET

This is the smallest caviar of all. It has a delicious texture as a fish, and the caviar eggs are similar to Sevruga. It is on the scale of the less expensive caviars (well, on the scale of caviars, anyway).

There are some substitutes for sturgeon caviar, such as salmon and trout caviar. Usually, the color of salmon caviar is a pale orange to a rich red. It's also quite delicious.

NUTRITION FACTS ABOUT CAVIAR

Caviar is not only a stylish, elegant food; it's high in nutritional content as well. Caviar is a rich source of calcium, protein, and vita-mins D and B12. Unfortunately, though, it is very high in sodium. Pre-serving caviar usually requires a large quantity of salt to keep the eggs in good shape.

When caviar is prepared, it usually stays in closed tins because it is so delicate that it can easily be destroyed. This is important for cav-iar lovers: the eggs need to maintain their texture and wholeness.

Caviar can also be pasteurized, but then it has to be cooked slightly, which destroys the nutritional value and the texture. Every-thing from the caviar is used, resulting in broken, discolored, and smashed eggs, but they can be pressed and still used.

Serving and eating caviar

Caviar is usually served with a slice of toast or crackers without salt, because the caviar's already salty flavor takes precedence. It is usually reserved for high-profile parties and entertainment. In the best restaurants around the world that serve caviar, it is usually served with red onions (which are usually diced), chives, eggs (with the whites and yolk separated), and crème fraiche, which is a heavy cream.

Caviar is traditionally eaten *directly* from the skin, holding it between the index finger and the thumb.

Never eat caviar with a regular utensil; it shouldn't touch metal, not even silver or gold. Metal can add a strong iron taste, which can develop into an unpleasant oxidation. If you're a true caviar lover, you probably already have a spoon or a fork made of shell and mother-of-pearl, which is an excellent choice.

Usually, the caviar is served in a little bowl that is placed in a bigger bowl full of crushed ice. If you don't have a bowl, you can place the caviar in a shell.

According to etiquette rules, we shouldn't have more than two spoons of caviar.

HOW DO YOU PAIR CAVIAR WITH ALCOHOL?

Caviar is best served with vodka to enhance the flavor. Remember that caviar comes from very cold regions (around the Caspian Sea) where vodka is a popular drink.

Caviar can also be paired with Brut champagne, and it needs to be Ultra Brut. Usually, champagne has a sweet taste, and this can create an odd mixture with the salty caviar flavor. Vodka has an extremely pure taste, and this can distinguish the caviar flavor perfectly, so your best choice is vodka.

Some people drink beer with caviar, but for exquisite occasions, the preferable choice is vodka or champagne.

A caviar set is my signature gift for every stylish occasion. This is something that many people wouldn't consider bringing as a gift, but it's actually inexpensive, and you can find it easily on Amazon.

Taking care of your caviar set is easy. Hand wash it without any heavy detergents, which can damage the set. Use a gentle soap, and don't dry it in the dishwasher. Dry it with a soft cloth.

CHAPTER SIX

DRESS CODE

Dressing well is a form of good manners.

—Tom Ford

Dressing well and appropriately is an art and a way of living for many people. I personally have been in a lot of uncomfortable situations because I was underdressed or I wasn't dressed up for the occasion, and my evening or event was ruined because I didn't have the knowledge of what to wear. We all know how important the first impression is, and dressing well has a very high impact on our success in life and in business. We don't have to wear the most expensive or fashionable clothing, but we should be able to recognize what to wear for any occasion

In my book *The Sharpest Soft Skill*, I wrote about the power of knowing your suitable colors, the materials you should wear according to the seasons (and according to your psychic). I advised on how to pick up your clothes and how to take care of them. I wrote about choosing wisely between classic clothing vs. the new modern trends and much more. You will be able to learn about the different attires as well.

In *Posh Overnight*, we will learn a little bit regarding the high-end fashion required at particular events. Not everyone gets invited to black- or white-tie events, but sometimes we do get invited, and I would like you to be prepared for these situations. When you are ready, you will have an amazing experience, and you will feel like a million dollars! If we receive an invitation for a high-profile event, on the top of the invitation will be indicated the dress code we should follow. I will give you a brief idea of what to wear and what to look for while dressing for formal events.

BLACK TIE OR WHITE TIE

BLACK TIE

For the gentlemen:

- Tuxedo with elegant silk lapels or a fine jacket
- Matching tapered (narrow) trousers (no belt)
- Black silk bow tie
- White dress shirt made of fine materials such as silk or cotton, well pressed

- Shoes in the evening should be black patent. During the day, black leather (not shiny) is the right choice.
- The socks should be black as well, made of a thin, elegant material.
- Cufflinks

For the ladies:

- A dress is one of the most appropriate choices for high-profile events. The dress should be a long, full-length dress. We need to make sure that the dress is not too long for us: it should be the appropriate length according to our height. If it is too long, we won't be comfortable walking around, and we might even fall, which can be a very uncomfortable situation. Always try the dress on at least a few days before you go to the event. Also, we need to make sure that the texture and the fabric are suitable for the high-profile celebration or event. My preferred textures are silk and velvet. You can even add a lot of sparkle—something different and shiny, remarkable and exquisite.
- We should carry a clutch—something small and elegant for the most necessary things.
- The shoes need to be also elegant, dressy, and beautiful, complementing the dress.
- This is an occasion when we can accentuate our makeup: casual hair and makeup styles won't compliment the glam of the event. You should be visible.
- Jewelry must be elegant, but we can also wear something more extravagant, depending on the dress choice. If the dress has a simple look, then we can make a statement by going more "flashy" with the jewelry. Just keep it classy at the same time.

WHITE TIE

For the gentlemen:

- Black tuxedo with tails
- Matching trousers with double satin strips
- Stiff-front white shirt; shirt with wing collar and cummerbund
- The bow tie is white.
- Marcela vest, white
- The shoes are the same as for black tie (shined patent), and the socks are thin and elegant.
- A pocket watch is an elegant accessory, even for our modern-day living. Also, white studs—shiny but subtle.

For the ladies:

- This is the moment for you to shine. You should put your best foot forward.
- Always wear a dress. Avoid two-piece ensembles. The dress should be full length, very elegant, and distinct. We can wear also gloves, which should create a stylish, exquisite look. If you get introduced to other guests during the event, do not remove your gloves. It is perfectly fine to shake hands while wearing the gloves. They are part of the outfit.

- The hair should be *up*. Usually when the hair is styled down, it shows a bit of a more relaxed look.
- We shouldn't wear watches for such formal occasions; we can, but only if the watch resembles a bracelet and matches our jewelry.

This is a just a survival introduction for your next big event—just a few elements to remember. Less is always more, and elegance is timeless. Your refined attitude, class, and finesse will complement everything you wear.

CHAPTER SEVEN

TRAVEL ETIQUETTE FUNDAMENTALS

Like all great travellers, I have seen more than I remember,
and remember more than I have seen.

—Benjamin Disraeli

I n our constantly changing world, you probably travel a lot. Most business is conducted globally, which requires more knowledge than ever before. We need to know strict rules and regulations while we are traveling abroad so we can avoid unpleasant situations at all times. Traveling should be educational, pleasant, and exciting, even while we are traveling for business! When I travel for work, I always try to have a good time, and I do my research before I travel. Organization takes time, so be prepared, and exercise patience.

AIR TRAVEL

LET'S START AT THE AIRPORT.

How you pack your luggage really matters. I don't know about you, but I start my luggage preparation a few days before I travel. As a matter of fact, I always have my basic travel supplies ready in my carry-on (I travel constantly, so this helps me avoid a lot of stress).

Have your passport ready; make sure that it's not going to expire in the six months after you start to travel. Be organized! Remember, the way we do one thing is the way we do everything. I usually use brightly colored luggage because it's easy for me to spot on the baggage carousel almost immediately, and it keeps me from accidentally taking someone else's luggage.

Check the requirements of your plane carrier, and follow the rules. There is nothing more annoying than being held up by security because of silly mistakes. The security guidelines might change pretty often, so always make sure to check before you travel.

There will be always a weight limit for your luggage, so make sure to check the weight at home or when you first get to the airport. It's very difficult to rearrange your entire suitcase at the last minute, trying to fit everything in and in between. Airplanes charge a lot of money for overweight luggage, and I'm sure you don't want to spend extra because of poor preparation.

When you finally get your boarding pass and you can go through the security line, follow the rules. Most of the time, you'll have to take off your shoes, so wear comfortable ones that are easy to remove. If you carry your laptop, remove it from the case, and be ready to comply with the directions from the security agent.

Smile when you reach the plane and meet the flight attendants! Greet them politely; if you aren't sure where your seat is, you can request their assistance.

WHAT SHOULD YOU WEAR WHILE TRAVELING?

You should be comfortable, but you should also be appropriately dressed. Many times, especially on a business trip, you might meet a business partner or a client at the airport, and you have to create a good impression, so try and look sharp.

You should wear clothes that don't wrinkle easily, and avoid light colors—they show dirt more easily. Try to wear fabrics that are suitable for the season. This might be a little tricky at times, because if you're traveling from Europe to California in December, the weather will change quite dramatically.

I personally don't like to see flip-flops anywhere, except at the beach, but they can be a comfortable choice when you're already sitting on the airplane. Go ahead and rest your feet in some comfortable flip-flops or fluffy socks.

Yoga pants are very popular choice. If you wear yoga pants, try to avoid any with tacky phrase or pictures on them.

Your jewelry doesn't have to be your most expensive, especially since you might have to remove it frequently at checkpoints, and you don't want to lose it. Less is more in this case. Jewelry that won't set off the metal detector is your best bet.

Don't forget to carry a jacket, even during the summer months. Airplanes are always cold. Attendants might offer a little blanket, or you can ask for one, but I personally always try to be prepared for this situation with at least a light jacket.

Always carry wet wipes: you want to feel fresh and comfortable. You can use them for your face and hands, to remove makeup easily, and, in general, for just about anything.

Don't wear strong cologne or perfume, because this can trigger allergic reactions in many people. The same goes for hair spray: just don't use too much.

How to behave on the plane

Being on an airplane for hours can be extremely frustrating and stressful especially if other people are inconsiderate. As a passenger, you always need to try to treat the rest of the passengers and the staff with respect and consideration. When you move through the aisles, you should exercise patience when people move more slowly than you might like. Don't rush them, roll your eyes, or make rude comments. You'll get to your seat in no time.

Your seat will have a reclining option, which is there for your comfort, but you should use it politely. Briefly check with the person behind you to see if it is convenient for them as well. They might have their table down, and you could cause them to spill their drinks. Also, you should do it very gently, because the person behind you might have their head resting on the back of your seat, so you should try to be careful.

The person in the middle seat always has the right to rest their arms on the armrest. They have the worst, most uncomfortable seat. Even if they don't use the armrest, you should ask them first if they might use it before you do.

Good hygiene is extremely important while you travel. We might assume that because people on the plane don't know us, we don't even need to take a shower or brush our teeth. This is the wrong approach, because we always need to try and look put together while we travel.

I personally have an issue with loud passengers. I dislike noise, and I can be easily offended by it. If you know that you have a loud family, remember not to inconvenience the rest of the passengers at all times. Don't scream at your children. If they aren't seated next to you, you can go and "visit" from time to time, but don't block the aisle, and don't hold your conversations on top of another passenger. It is very rude and inconsiderate.

If you'd like to sleep on the flight, you should book a window seat. If you are sitting by the aisle, the rest of the passengers will have to try and jump over you to be able to stretch or use the restroom.

Always be very careful when you drink on the plane, because you don't want to inconvenience the rest of the plane with rude or outrageous behavior. Limit your drinks.

Treat the staff nicely; they will be busy throughout the flight serving all the passengers. Don't make outrageous requests, and always be pleasant and polite.

If you'd like to be considerate of the great job the flight attendants do, you can always write a thoughtful note to their headquarters or even post something thoughtful on the airline's Facebook page. This can go a long way, and they could even get a raise or a promotion. We always should be grateful!

If the flight attendant is personable, polite, attentive, and warm, you should give him or her recognition.

Respecting different cultures while traveling

We always need to read about the rules and regulations in other countries we travel to because, in some cases, not doing so could be physically dangerous, or we can just be perceived as inconsiderate, rude, and obnoxious.

Rules while traveling in Muslim countries – I work with people from this region of the world, and I know that, for them, religion is above protocol. Even if we don't observe the same religion, we should be always nice and respectful. We need to observe the local norms.

In the image above, I am visiting Sheikh Saied's Mosque in Abu Dhabi, and I am wearing the traditional local attire required to enter the mosque. It was an incredibly beautiful experience.

We always need to remember, when visiting another country and culture, to show respect and humility. We are visitors, and respect will be reciprocated. Let civility prevail.

There in the UAE in July, certainly you can imagine that it was probably 110 degrees. But I really, really wanted to see the majestic mosque, so I followed the rules. Women are required to cover their head with a head scarf and wear an abaya. In some countries, such as Saudi Arabia, this is a requirement all the time, but in the UAE, you don't have to wear them at all times.

Even so, respectful clothing is a must, because we do not want to offend our hosts. For example, we should stay away from revealing clothes that show a lot of skin; also, shorts are not a preferable choice.

If you travel during Ramadan, you should consider the fact that it is in bad taste to eat and drink in front of the people who are fasting. They might tell you that it's okay because, for them, it's polite to make you feel comfortable, but you should refrain from being provocative in this regard. Also, you might see people praying at the airport; don't stare. Just try to understand the customs.

When you get to the hotel, you have to consider tipping the hotel staff. Housekeeping is essential for a pleasant stay, so it is good etiquette to leave a couple of dollars on the pillow with a thank-you note. You should be consistent, because the staff changes, and you should show appreciation for all of them.

CHAPTER EIGHT

ETIQUETTE FOR CULTURAL ACTIVITIES

BALLET, OPERA, AND THEATER

Around the world, ballet is considered one of the most formal cultural activities. Everything is so precise, beautiful, and elegant, and you'll never be the same after you witness such an event. I remember visiting Moscow; one of the first events we attended was the *Nutcracker*, and I was absolutely mesmerized!

We always need to consider the fact that these events are pretty formal, but not always. For example, there is no official dress code in The Royal Opera House—you can dress up or down. But I strongly suggest that you consider the dress code and always dress one level up—in this case, maybe more than one.

Dressing appropriately is always a good way to start the evening. Definitely stay away from jeans and t-shirts; you would like to show respect for the art that will be presented, the people around you, and for yourself.

In the picture below, I'm attending a performance of Verdi's *Othello* at the Royal Opera at Covent Garden in London, and I really wanted to look exquisite.

You should arrive promptly or 15–30 minutes early, especially because you will be sitting with other people in your row. If you arrive late for the event, it's likely that you won't be allowed to enter until the intermission or another appropriate break in the performance.

Don't let the majestic venue intimidate you. It is always a pleasure to hear and see outstanding talent from all over the world. This will be an unforgettable experience that will stay in your heart and memory forever.

Hats, such as baseball caps or any kind of sports hat, are not permissible. Do not wear sneakers or sportswear.

You will see ladies wearing evening gowns, and they will look absolutely gorgeous. This is their special opportunity to dress beautifully in our relaxed, casual world.

Men can wear a nice jacket or black-tie attire. Be extremely elegant, especially if the lady is wearing something elegant herself.

Always use the coat room before you're seated; you want to be comfortable and relaxed inside, and it's hard to move freely when you're wearing a lot of clothes.

Ladies should carry a small clutch, not a big purse. Once, when I was coming directly from a business meeting, I successfully tried to get an opera-ready look, but I didn't have my clutch at the time. I didn't want to be late for the occasion, so I went with my regular purse. Sometimes we have to choose our battles.

If you are very late, you might not be allowed to sit in your seat because the movement would be distracting, not only for the people around you but also for the artists, especially if your seat is somewhere up front. If you are late and you have to pass the people on your row, say "Excuse me," and always do it face to face, not with your back to them. If your seat is in the middle of the row, don't wait until the last minute. Take your seat before the rest of the row, because you don't want to inconvenience them. Don't go back and forward while you should be sitting.

If you have a program, read it before the performance starts. Turning the pages could be loud and intrusive for the rest of the people around you.

YOUR PHONE

It's too bad that we need to have rules regarding phones all the time. Your phone needs to be in silent mode, and don't send messages; the light from the screen can be very annoying for the rest of the people. Always keep your conversations to a minimum, and use a gentle, low tone of voice.

Food and drinks are highly inappropriate during your visit to the opera or the ballet. You will need to wait until the intermission to take care of what you need to: get food and drinks, use the restroom, make phone calls, and have conversations.

The reward for every artist is the applause. You have to show the artist that you are grateful for their incredible performance, but you should do it appropriately! In the opera house, applause usually comes at the end of an aria and at the end of each act. Pay attention: even if you don't understand much about opera, follow the rest of the audience, and they'll give you the cue about when to clap. Clapping during an act, especially while the artists are singing, can be pretty disturbing for everybody. That's why you refrain from clapping in the middle and wait until the end of the aria.

No pictures!

The audience is usually not permitted to take any photographs. You should follow the rules at all times. It is highly intrusive and inappropriate to be warned during the performance that you can't use your camera under any circumstances and you still continue to do so.

Intermission time!

This is a very pleasant time for many people who are not used to the art of the opera or the ballet ☺.

This is the opportunity for you to have a drink or a light snack, fix your hair, and just walk around.

Be careful with your drinks, and be mindful of the quantity. You can walk around and see the beautiful portraits by many great artists, feel the atmosphere of the exquisite lifestyle, and enjoy the enormous talent.

When the time is getting closer to get back to your seat, you'll hear a warning signal, which you definitely won't be able to miss because it's very strong and distinctive. Return to your seat and continue to absorb the beauty of the finest arts in life, opera and ballet.

Again, if your seat is in the middle of the row, don't be late. If you were late for the beginning of the performance and you're about to be late again after intermission, then you really need to work on your punctuality (and maybe your consideration), because you're showing that you could care less about the rest of the people.

THE END

After the performance is over, it's time for you to applaud loudly, happily, gratefully, and show your appreciation to the performers! You can even stand up while you are applauding. If it was a great performance, everybody else will be standing anyway.

Do not leave early under any circumstances, especially if you have the middle seat. You will have to wait patiently until everybody leaves (or at least the people before you).

While leaving the building, don't rush, push, or show frustration or irritation. This will bring an unnecessarily unpleasant mood to the people around you, both those you know and those you don't.

MUSEUMS AND ART GALLERIES

National History Museum, London

Many of us love visiting museums, expanding our knowledge about global events that perhaps changed the world in a certain way or were part of the history of a particular country. We may be fortunate enough to see amazing art everywhere we go!

Etiquette is used or abused everywhere we go and in everything we do.

There are a few particular rules we should always keep in mind while visiting such venues. Let me remind you: from the Louvre in Paris to the smallest museum with just ten exhibits, your behavior should be always cordial.

DO NOT TOUCH.

On many occasions, we will be so mesmerized by the beauty and the significant value of the exhibits that we will be tempted to touch them. We don't need to be reminded that we cannot do so.

We can look from a slight distance, read the information next to the exhibited painting or craft, admire it, and move on. Many of the exhibits are hundreds of years old, and we would like to make sure that they will be preserved for the generations after us.

BE QUIET.

If you're visiting a museum or gallery with a large group, don't shout at the people with you. You should be quiet, because other people (or even your group) might have a guide, and they want to be able to hear the information about the particular painting or sculpture.

Do not join a group without permission.

Many times, you might be really interested in the information that's being presented to a group in the venue, but if you aren't part of that group, you shouldn't just join without permission. They might let you know that you are not wanted there, and you want to save this embarrassment.

CELL PHONES

You already know the rule about the cell phones, but it is a necessary reminder every time. Do not use your cell phone inside the museum. Do not take any phone calls. Just leave the phone alone. This is a public place; everybody would like to enjoy it, and cell phones are extremely disruptive.

PICTURES

For the exhibit below, I specifically asked if I could take a picture, because the folklore clothing is pretty old, and I didn't want it to get damaged by my humble photography.

This is Bulgarian traditional attire, 200 hundred years old.

If there is a rule against taking pictures, then you shouldn't take pictures, under any circumstances! Some of the world's best-known museums receive millions of visitors every year, and the brightness of cameras flashing can slowly but surely destroy an exhibit. This is something to consider at all times. In general, if there are mandatory rules regarding a particular venue, there is obviously a reason for them. They sometimes might not make sense to us, but they are important for saving delicate pieces.

STAYING IN FRONT OF THE ART FOR AN INCREDIBLY LONG TIME

Many people say that they get recharged in a museum or an art gallery, which makes a lot of sense. The only issue we might have with that is if they block the art for an increasingly long period of time, people will pile in front of it to see it as well. We have to be very mindful that this is a public space, and everyone would love to see the art. Usually, you might be able to see the art from a particular distance and at a particular angle. Do so, and move silently, because the person after you would love to enjoy it as well.

DO NOT SIT ON THE EXPOSED ART OBJECTS!

This is exactly what was written (see the picture below) in one of the museums in Dubai I had the opportunity to visit.

This exhibit was representing the beginning of the UAE and can introduce the world to the humble bedouin life. If we all pay attention and follow etiquette, this will be preserved for generations to come.

Sometimes we can get extremely tired because we have been walking for so long, trying to absorb as much as we can in a short time, and we can get very tired. This doesn't mean we should take a break by sitting on the exhibited objects, hoping that no one can see us. No, everybody can, and it looks extremely inconsiderate. You definitely can ruin the exhibited art.

DO NOT EAT OR DRINK INSIDE THE MUSEUM.

In bigger museums, you will usually find designated places to have a nice breakfast, lunch, or even dinner. Make sure to use this space. Do not eat or drink inside the venue. It is not only highly inappropriate but can also damage the art pieces. In addition, we would like to keep the place clean for everyone to enjoy after we leave.

WATCH YOUR KIDS.

As parents, we can be challenged at times because our kids may want to see something completely different than what we want to see. Do not let them run around, because this can be very difficult, not only for you but also for the people around you. Also, make sure they are not hiding somewhere behind the art pieces. This could be very dangerous, and they can get hurt.

CHAPTER NINE

POLO MATCH ETIQUETTE

R oyal Ascot is Britain's most celebrated race meeting, attracting many of the world's elite racehorses to compete for millions of dollars in prize money. The five-day event is known for its lucrative spectacle, where fashion, style, socializing, and fine dining are at their pinnacle.

Meanwhile, in the United States, we enjoy the Kentucky Derby, and every year in May, we get ready for the opening of polo season here in San Diego. I would like to share some information about this very old sport and the etiquette norms we should follow while attending polo matches. You might be invited, and you need to own it!

The term "polo" originates from the Tibetan word "pulu," which means ball. Polo is an ancient team sport that is played on horseback: players score points by using long mallets to drive a ball into the opponent's goal. Polo most likely began in Persia and spread to other parts of Southern and Central Asia. The game was very popular during China's Tang Dynasty, as we can see from its depiction in paintings and statues from that period.

ATTIRE

Polo matches are often seen as highly anticipated spectacles and fashion statements. At the same time, it depends very much on what level of game you are watching. In the United States, most polo matches are casual, family events. However, for finals and championship games, men should wear jackets or suits, and women should wear summery, fresh, classy-looking dresses. Bright colors and floral printed dresses are favored. And of course, the oh-so-popular big beautiful hats!

Because polo clubs have a lot of grass and unpaved areas, stilettos won't be your best choice, especially if you plan to participate in the Divot Stomp.

MINDING YOUR MANNERS

- Spectators shouldn't sit on top of the fences, because this is an elegant and classy event.
- The big difference between polo and other sports is that spectators do not cheer loudly for their favorite player; it could distract or frighten the ponies. Soft applause is acceptable.
- Parents must supervise their children at all times, because it can be very dangerous if they run onto the turf.

PONIES

We do address the horses as ponies, and each player can have more than one. The polo pony is professionally trained and carefully selected for speed, stamina, and agility. At the same time, one of the most important characteristics is the pony's temperament; he must remain responsive under pressure and easily controlled.

DIVOT STOMP

During this traditional halftime activity for attendees, spectators spill on to the playing field (called the "pitch") to stomp down any of the turf that has been kicked up during the game by the ponies' hooves. It is a very large field, so if you don't join the Divot Stomp, it might be a good idea to carry binoculars to get a better view of the fun.

SEATING ARRANGEMENTS

Polo matches usually have a couple of seating arrangements: bleacher seating and members' enclosure. Spectators in bleacher seating bring their own picnic lunches, while club members enjoy a lavish sit-down lunch, afternoon tea, and endless champagne.

I hope this will get you ready for an amazing time at your next (or your first) polo match, and don't forget to have fun!

CHAPTER TEN

THE BRITISH INSTITUTION: TEA

There are few hours in life more agreeable than the hour dedicated to the ceremony known as afternoon tea.

—Henry James

According to "Victorian Tea Parties," a very popular, beautiful blog, there is a legend that the drinking of tea originated from the time of Emperor Shennong (in 2737 BC), who was visiting a distant region with his court. He stopped for a break. His servants started boiling water on the fire, and a dried leave fell into the water. He tasted the water, which became colorful from the leaves, and he found out that it tasted delicious and refreshing, so they made more! The story goes that this was the beginning of tea drinking.

In China, the preparation and cultivation of tea became a way of life.

Later on, in the sixteenth century, tea made its way to Europe, and it became a very fashionable and expensive beverage.

Tea was first traded in England in the seventeenth century by the merchant Thomas Garway. Tea became extremely popular even though it was sold at an ultra-high price.

TRADITIONAL AFTERNOON TEA

The afternoon tea started when Anna, Seventh Duchess of Bedford, wanted to bridge the gap between lunch and dinner. This became an extremely popular affair, and people started organizing tea parties for status and prestige. It was popular in the upper class because it wasn't cheap.

If you are a tea lover, one of the destinations that must be on your bucket list is The Savoy in London. This hotel is one of the luxury trademarks of the city. The Savoy serves one of London's finest traditional afternoon teas.

You will have to make a reservation at least a few months in advance, because visitors from all over the world come to see this iconic place. Some of the most famous guests have included Frank Sinatra,

Charlie Chaplin, Marilyn Monroe, Elizabeth Taylor, Winston Churchill, and many others. You will be very pleased to be able to be a part of this experience.

The tradition is that the establishment cannot serve thirteen people, and that's why, in a situation such as this, they have a mascot called Casper.

Traditional afternoon tea at The Savoy

The traditional afternoon tea takes place between 3 and 5 p.m. and includes:

- *Finger Sandwiches* – The sandwiches are usually served without the crust on thin slices of bread, gently buttered. The bread can be different varieties, such as olive bread, white bread, brown bread, spinach bread, and more.
  What can be used on the sandwich: classic egg salad, smoked salmon, cucumbers, chicken, mozzarella cheese, basil, and much more.

The tea usually starts with the sandwiches, because they are savory, and this can boost the appetite.

- *Freshly baked scones* – British shortbreads, which are sweet, but in moderation.
- *Afternoon pastries* are the sweet dessert, which can include everything from eclairs to delicious coffee cakes.

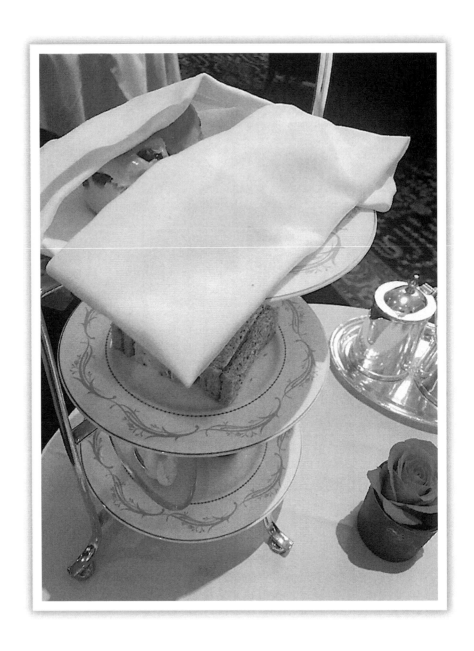

TRADITIONAL HIGH TEA

This arose during the Industrial Revolution, and it was a regular meal, served as a supper. The high tea was a completely different event compared to the traditional afternoon tea, which was more for entertainment purposes and was kept much lighter because it was the bridge between the lunch and the supper.

The traditional high tea was popular among the working class and included heavy foods such as:

- Kidney pies, roast beef, and sausages
- Bread and butter
- Jam
- Cheese
- Pickles
- Cakes

When you are visiting a tea party, it usually has the same requirements as any other event. You have to be invited, introduced, and made aware if there's a guest of honor.

The hostess will pour tea into your cup, and you will be the one who will be adding sugar, lemon, milk, or whatever your preferences might be.

The hostess will perhaps ask you if you would like the tea strong or weak, and if the answer is "strong," she will fill your teacup three-quarters full. If you prefer it weak, she will fill your cup only halfway.

You can choose if you would like milk, sugar, or lemon. Usually we put the sugar in first because it should dissolve easily, and after that we can put in lemon or milk. Obviously, milk and lemon do not go hand in hand.

Never blow on the tea if it is too hot. You will have to wait a little to let it cool off. The spoon goes on the saucer, never on the table after has been used.

If you pour tea for your guests, you should be mindful of holding the teapot's lid.

When you need to stir the sugar, always use the teaspoon gently by moving it inside the cup, back and forth, following an imagined arc. Try to avoid loud noises while you are doing so.

Also, something seen as a faux pas is having your pinkie hanging out. It is not acceptable.

Tea is largely popular as loose leaves, because the flavor can be really distinguished and unmistakable. Some teas are rather rich, while others have a softer, lighter flavor. It doesn't matter what kind of tea is preferred: the rules are the same for every kind of tea.

Of course, if you use loose tea leaves, you will certainly need to use a tea strainer.

On very formal occasions, loose leaves are highly preferred, but in our daily lives, tea bags are extremely popular.

Thomas Sullivan, a merchant from New York, invented the tea bag by accident in 1908 when he started sending tea to his clients in small bags for them to try the varieties of tea he was offering. After that, tea bags became wildly popular, and his invention took the world by storm.

When you make your tea from a tea bag, gently place the tea bag in the cup with the hot water, and leave it for a small amount of time (or longer, depending on how strong you prefer the tea to be). When you are done, simply take out the silky package and leave it in the saucer or on a plate that might be on the table for used tea bags.

Dear friends,

I am so glad that you stayed with me to the end of this brief survival guide on social etiquette, and I hope you feel much more comfortable while you are visiting different types of events all over the world. The main message is: raise your standards, learn a lot, travel safely as much as you can, and do not feel intimidated while visiting high-profile events.

The world was my oyster but I used the wrong fork.

—Oscar Wilde

And use the right fork while "eating oysters"!

Much love and success!

Maryanne

Made in the USA
Columbia, SC
16 November 2022

71391360R00065